I0421223

Manipulation Manual

Your Survival Guide for Outwitting Emotional Manipulators and Pathological Liars in Your Relationships

© Copyright 2015 - All rights reserved.

This document is geared towards providing exact and reliable information in regards to the topic and issue covered. The publication is sold with the idea that the publisher is not required to render accounting, officially permitted, or otherwise, qualified services. If advice is necessary, legal or professional, a practiced individual in the profession should be ordered.

- From a Declaration of Principles which was accepted and approved equally by a Committee of the American Bar Association and a Committee of Publishers and Associations.

In no way is it legal to reproduce, duplicate, or transmit any part of this document in either electronic means or in printed format. Recording of this publication is strictly prohibited and any storage of this document is not allowed unless with written permission from the publisher. All rights reserved.

The information provided herein is stated to be truthful and consistent, in that any liability, in terms of inattention or otherwise, by any usage or abuse of any policies, processes, or directions contained within is the solitary and utter responsibility of the recipient reader. Under no circumstances will any legal responsibility or blame be held against the publisher for any reparation, damages, or monetary loss due to the information herein, either directly or indirectly.

Respective authors own all copyrights not held by the publisher.

The information herein is offered for informational purposes solely, and is universal as so. The presentation of the information is without contract or any type of guarantee assurance.

The trademarks that are used are without any consent, and the publication of the trademark is without permission or backing by the trademark owner. All trademarks and brands within this book are for clarifying purposes only and are the owned by the owners themselves, not affiliated with this document.

Table of Contents

Introduction

I want to thank you and congratulate you for purchasing the book, "*Manipulation Manual: Your Survival Guide for Outwitting Emotional Manipulators and Pathological Liars in Your Relationships*".

This book contains proven steps and strategies on how to free yourself from free yourself from the clutches of master manipulators and regain your sense of self again.

We all have that one manipulative person in our lives that we can't seem to get rid of. While dysfunctional relationships may come in many forms, a manipulative relationship can change you completely.

Manipulative people have a way of wasting your time, resources, energy, and even your own appreciation for yourself. When this happens, it's just a matter of time before you realize that you've allowed them to go too far and that there's nothing left for you.

This is why it's important that you actually understand what manipulative relationships are and how they can affect your quality of life. You'll be surprised that the thing you call love may not be love after all.

This book is designed to help you understand what manipulative relationships are about. From what they are exactly to the physical symptoms you may experience when you're caught up in one, this book is packed with insights on how to shake off unhealthy relationships for good.

Are you Vulnerable to being Manipulated?

We can all become victims of manipulators at one point or another. Whether by people we consider as friends, lovers, or even family members, it's easy to fall into the trap of a master manipulator.

Manipulative relationships may come in many different forms, but at the end of the day, it leaves you feeling worn out and helpless. Most people will live their lives not knowing that they're already being manipulated, and frankly, that's what makes the situation even more difficult to get out of. Many people end up in manipulative relationships not because they like being manipulated, but because they honestly don't see any way out.

Manipulative relationships are often extremely one sided and only advantageous to the one who holds all the manipulation. While it's not as obvious as being in a toxic relationship, manipulative relationships work on a higher level of manipulation and deceit. To know whether you are already being manipulated, or if you're vulnerable to becoming a victim of a manipulative relationship, try checking with yourself if you possess any of the following traits.

You only feel loved when you try to meet the needs of others

There's nothing wrong with being nice to other people. In fact, kindness is one of the few traits that make life worthwhile. But if you're only being kind because it makes you feel wanted or loved, then you might have the tendency to take it a bit too far. If you always find yourself wanting to please others at your own expense, it's time to quit that habit. You might be doing everyone else a favor, except yourself.

You never say No

One of the best things that you can do for yourself is to set up the appropriate boundaries in your relationships. This helps keep your sense of self intact, as well as let people know what you stand for. You can't set healthy boundaries if you keep on giving into what other people want. Even if you're afraid of conflict, you need to learn how to say no and protect yourself from being manipulated. By asserting your sense of self, you not only regain your control, but you also send out the message that you're not someone that can easily be taken advantage of.

You seldom let your negative emotions out

While dealing with negative emotions is never pleasant, you need to find healthy ways to let it all out. When you go to extremes of hiding your negative emotions in just to avoid confrontation, you're only setting yourself up to be manipulated even more. When you try too hard to keep it all positive on the outside, all that pent up anger and frustration will leave you rotting on the inside. Master manipulators have a way of using this trait to their advantage. All they have to do is push you to the edge and agitate you to get their way.

You constantly try to win the approval of other people

There's nothing wrong about wanting to feel accepted, but that doesn't mean that you should work on being accepted all the time – BY EVERYONE. If you have an underlying fear or being abandoned or rejected, this could make you vulnerable to the most common manipulation tactic there is. The manipulator will give you the approval you crave for, but will quickly withdraw it if you don't give it to what he or she wants you to do.

You have no clear idea of who you are

If you don't know who you are, it will be hard for you to fight for what you want. When you don't have a strong sense of self, it becomes hard for you to make decisions for yourself. Having a clear sense of who you are and what you value will empower you to set clear boundaries. Not having any boundaries only makes you an easy target for the manipulators out there.

The Concept of Manipulation and Influence

The concept of manipulation may seem very similar to the concept of influence, but if you're going to look deeper into it, they're completely different from each other. Influence is based on honest and direct communication, while manipulation is based on deceit and covert agendas. Influence upholds the other person's integrity, while manipulation is designed to break down a person's confidence and security. Influence plays a crucial role in strengthening our bond with one another, while manipulation aims cut off the personal ties that connect us to each other.

You can't free yourself from the clutches of manipulation without first understanding and accepting your role in the equation. It may be difficult to admit to your weaknesses, but once you become aware of how you're contributing to the circumstances, it will be easier for you to put an end to that. By understanding how exactly you make yourself vulnerable to manipulative relationships, you'll be able to take the necessary steps to finally get out of the situation.

The 10 Types of Manipulators

Have you ever been a victim of emotional abuse or found yourself in an abusive relationship? If you're sick and tired of dealing with the mess and you just want a way out, the good news is, you have more power over your situation than you believe. While you may not have the power to change how people act around you, you can however change how you see them and it all starts with knowing what type of manipulator you're dealing with.

Before you can take this situation head on, you need to recognize the different traits of the most common types of manipulators. Even though we may have our own level of tolerance for manipulative people, it's easy to point out specific behavioral patterns that can act as your red flag. Here's a list of the 10 types of manipulators you need to avoid at all cost!

The Victim: This type of manipulator has a way of making everything about him or her. It doesn't matter if you're going through issues of your own, the victim will find ways to gain the sympathy of others. In order to avoid taking responsibility over his or her own actions when things go wrong, this type of emotional manipulator is quick to turn the tables around and make it seem like he or she was the victim all along.

The Weakling: The weakling may seem all frail and powerless on the outside, but inside, this type of manipulator is hungry for power. The weakling uses different tactics to gain considerable power over their target. From seemingly harmless compliments to emotional blackmail, the weakling has mastered the art of getting their needs met without coming off as self-centered.

The Expert: this person is fueled by the need to always be on higher ground than others. It doesn't matter what setting they're in or what the circumstances are, the expert needs to come out on top, almost all the time. Some may see this behavior as narcissistic, while others look at it as arrogance, but what sets the expert on a higher plane is the fact that he or she is completely aware of this need to always be better. When pushed to the edge, the expert will resort to insults and put downs to manipulate others.

The Defensive: The defensive will use outbursts of anger to avoid being confronted. Even when they're caught in the act, they will find ways to divert the attention from their mistakes. They will shield themselves from accusations and derail the issue using every dirty trick in the book. The defensive is not someone to engage in combat with.

The Conqueror: just like an old world conqueror, the conqueror will set strategies in place in order to control people within their range. They will create alliances with key personalities in order to deal with those who stand in their way. They may seem friendly in the beginning, even using compliments to create a bond with their victims, but once the bond has been made, they will then execute their plan for control.

The Projector: the projector likes to blame others for their own shortcomings or character flaws. They rarely take responsibility over their mistakes and will often use lies and denial to defend their own egos. While some projectors haven't the slightest idea of what they're doing, most projectors rarely care about the consequences of their actions.

The Flirt: this person uses flirtation to manipulate people into giving them what they want. Seen as very superficial people, they make the most out of their physical looks to gain control over people. Even when they're not seen as very attractive, the flirts will resort to sex to gain power and control. They have a high regard for themselves and have that air of self-entitlement. They feel very much in their element when they see that they're destroying relationships.

The Innocent: the innocents use lies and half-truths as their main weapon and will go to extremes to gain full control. They often come off as innocent and defenseless, but deep down, they have a way of slanting the truth to manipulate others to giving them what they want. They can create elaborate justifications so that people will believe them and their lies. The only time that they will come clean is when they've been backed into a corner, with no other way to go.

The Repeater: The repeater shows no remorse for their actions. They will continue to take advantage of their victims, even after they have already been caught. Once caught, they will look for other sways to manipulate others because clearly, giving up is not an option. They seldom back down until they finally get what they want.

The Intimidator: this type of manipulator sows fear in the hearts of their victims. They are demanding and very persistent in what they want. While most intimidators use their physical size to coerce people into handing over control, others intimidate using their intelligence and sometimes, aggression. Because they feel superior over others, they lack compassion for people in general.

Since these personalities have their own little quirks, they each demand their own approach. You can't deal with the intimidator the same way you would deal with a flirt. The key to dealing with manipulative people is to understand what exactly it is you're up against and create your own battle plan. Don't let all these manipulative personalities be the end of you because at the end of the day, you possess more power and control than you like to give yourself credit for.

How Manipulators Work and What You Can Do TODAY!

It's sad to think that there are countless people out there who are currently caught up in some form of emotional abuse. While most stay because they feel like they don't have a choice, there are some who unknowingly accept the manipulation that their partners regularly dish out.

When you allow emotional manipulation into your relationship, you allow others to take over your joy and control your personhood. This causes turmoil because it doesn't just cause chaos inside yourself, but it also sets the motion for a continuous cycle of emotional abuse.

Regardless of where you are in your life right now, if you're reading this, then you're probably a victim of some form of abusive or manipulative relationship. This form of relationship always starts with someone wanting to take control over another and finding ways to hold on to that control. It may not seem like you're being manipulated on the surface, but deep inside, it's already all sorts of chaos. That's generally how manipulators work. They will breed fear, self doubt, and trouble just to get what they want.

Manipulative relationships can come in all shapes and forms. It's not just your spouse who can hurt you this way. It can also be your parents, your children, your boss, and even your own best friend. This is why manipulative relationships isn't exactly that easy to get out of. You're not just dealing with the pain of a total stranger hurting you. You're dealing with the pain of someone special betraying you and taking advantage of you.

But despite what the manipulative people in your life have made you believe, you have all the power and control to get yourself out of manipulative relationships. You don't have to feel guilty about how you feel anymore, because you have all the right to your own emotions. You might feel helpless and alone right now, but once you start ridding yourself of all the manipulative people in your life, you will go back to feeling like yourself again.

The thing that you have to constantly remind yourself about manipulative relationships is that you're not responsible for how others feel about you. It's not your fault that they're like that so stop making excuses for their inexcusable behavior towards you. If you find yourself trying to justify their actions, you need to take a step back to see the entire picture. This is the only way that you'll be able to really see the effect manipulative people have on you.

You are however very much responsible for changing yourself. You still have a chance to change your life by changing the way you perceive the circumstances. This is the perfect time to do a self-evaluation of the things you need to change about yourself because once you understand what you need to change about yourself, it will be easier for you to back away from manipulative people.

Why are there manipulative people in the first place?

You probably have your own theory as to why manipulative people in your life are the way they are, but according to experts, it all boils to one thing: Self-absorption. Manipulative people are engrossed with having their wants, needs, and emotions met that they stop caring for anyone else. And since they're so absorbed with themselves, any effort that you make to try to change them will only go to waste. No matter how hard you try, they will always manage to bring the focus back to their own misery and lack. To compensate for the hole in their hearts, they resort to manipulating others.

Manipulation is often reinforced by the negativity that surrounds them. And since you can't fight fire with fire, you need to fight back with positivity. You need to establish yourself as the positive influence to counteract their negativity in your life. Although it's hard, you need to believe the best in people. If you want to reinforce positive behavior in people, you need to find ethical ways for them to see you as an ally, and not as enemy.

Changing your Approach

Taking on a positive outlook is actually simpler than you think. Instead of calling out a person for what he or she did wrong, you'll get better results by letting them know that you expect the best from them. Just by switching your approach, you'll be able to deal with manipulation without all the drama. No fighting, no shouting, just positive reinforcement.

Taking on the positive route is an effective means to manage different personalities. It may take some time, but commit to working on it and you'll be getting a positive response in no time.

The lessons that you will learn in this book is not exactly the temporary fix that you're hoping for. Rather, it's designed to guide you towards long term solutions that will help mend most human relationship.

Difficult people will always be a part of your life. But with enough perseverance and commitment, you can do your part in minimizing conflict in your life. Accept that everyone is different and that we all need to do our part in fostering a harmonious environment.

How Manipulators Can Affect You Physically

Studies show that people in general are more health conscious now than ever before. People are not only more conscious about the food they eat, but they also spend a lot of time working out and trying to look for products that will help them stay in great shape – inside and out.

But even with this recent obsession over giving their bodies the right care, there are very few people who are concerned about protecting themselves from manipulative relationships. They don't understand that the toxic emotions they feel inside can just be as harmful as the toxic chemicals that are present in the environment.

 In fact, being unhappy in abusive relationships has its way of manifesting itself to the body. When you allow yourself to be trapped in long periods of emotional abuse, it can lead to serious health problems.

There may be no such thing as a perfect relationship all the time, but that doesn't mean you should allow your body to take its toll. Whether you're dealing with a friend, a lover, a child, or a coworker, you need to start prioritizing yourself more. Here are a few questions you need to answer in order to properly understand your emotional state in your relationships.

- *Do you generally feel worn down and disinterested when you're with that person?*

- *Do you feel worse about yourself after spending time with that person?*

- *Do you feel like you're in danger, or threatened when you spend time with that person? Whether physically or emotionally?*

- *Do you see inconsistencies in how you're treated compared to how you treat him or her? How does that make you feel in general?*

- *Do you often find yourself wishing that he or she will change so that you'll feel happy and at peace?*

If you answered yes to any of these questions, then you need to reassess your relationship with the person again. You need to free yourself from the manipulation on order to see the relationship for what it really is.

If you're still not completely convinced about the negative effects that a manipulative relationship has on you, then it's time to watch out for the following physical symptoms. In case you still don't know, how you feel on the inside, has a way of manifesting on the outside.

Constant headaches

One clear sign that you're struggling in an unhealthy relationship is the constant headaches that you experience. Again, stress is probably the main culprit here. If your inner gut feeling is telling you things aren't working as they should, then there's a big chance that it isn't.

Noticeable weight loss or weight gain

Weight fluctuation is one of the most noticeable signs that you're in not in a good place emotionally. Whether your tendency is to eat more or eat less when under a lot of stress, expect your family and friends to take notice of any extreme weight changes. When they start to bring your weight difference to your attention, don't ignore it.

Stuffy nose

Noticing your immune system failing as you go deeper in that abusive relationship? That's definitely your body telling you that things aren't going right. You see the more anxious and depressed you are, the more susceptible your body is to contracting cold infections and flu attacks.

Dark under eye circles

Over thinking your circumstances and feeling less excited about your relationship is bound to end in many sleepless nights. If you begin to notice dark circles forming around your under eye area, it's time to get a clean break and just get away from it all. Those dark circles not only make you look tired, they also make you seem a lot older.

Frequent body pain

Anxiety causes tension in your muscles, leaving your extremities feeling achy and sore all over. When this happens, you need to get away as fast and as far as you can. Since pent up emotions can't go away by themselves, it's up to you to do something about it.

Stomach pain

Chronic stomach pain is another sign that you're experiencing too much anxiety and depression. And being around the other person isn't exactly going to help because the pain tends to get worse when you're around your partner. If you find yourself complaining about mysterious pain, then it's probably time to call it quits on the relationship – for your health's sake.

In order to live a healthy lifestyle, you need to be ready to make drastic changes – inside and out. As you have read, abusive relationships can affect your body in more ways than you would like to believe. Don't let deception and emotional manipulation prevent you from being happy and healthy. It's just not worth it.

How to Know if You're with a Pathological Liar

I don't think there's anyone who gets into a relationship with a pathological liar just for the heck of it. In fact, you won't exactly know that a person is a pathological liar until you catch him or her in the act. You'll only realize that that person has been lying to you after being betrayed. And even then, getting over that betrayal can be quite a challenge. You won't exactly find a sign that says "pathological liar" when you meet someone new. You'll only uncover his or her dirty secret once the damage has been done.

As with all kinds of relationships, a manipulative relationship starts off pretty harmless. But once you know each other a little better, you'll start to see how some things just don't add up. The inconsistencies will pile up and before you know it, you find yourself not knowing what to believe anymore. You'll feel a whole range of emotions, from confused to betrayed and complete lack of trust. Depending on how good of a liar the person is, it may take years before you notice that you have been a victim all this time.

Here's how to tell if you're having a relationship with someone who is a pathological liar.

You argue a lot because of inconsistencies

While it's completely normal to argue with a lover, but if you find yourself arguing nonstop over inconsistencies, then there's a major disconnect happening there. There will always be differences in relationships but if you're always struggling with inconsistent facts, then it's probably time that you call it quits.

You find wanting to spend less time with the person

Love relationships aren't always flowers and butterflies. There will be days when you just don't feel like being with the other person. But if you find yourself avoiding the other person because you're genuinely concerned about the other person's credibility, then something's definitely not right there.

You catch the person exaggerating a lot

We all have that tendency to exaggerate but if you find that the other person is doing it a lot, then that person might just be a compulsive liar. When a person exaggerates, it shows that he or she is has that tendency to twist the truth to his or her advantage. It doesn't matter if it's a small or big issue, if you catch a person exaggerating; it's time to rethink the relationship.

Your gut feeling always doubts what the person says

Another classic sign of a pathological liar is that your gut feeling doesn't always seem to agree with him or her. While you can't always rely on your gut feeling to decide whether you should still be with a person or nut, you inner sense can tell you if a person is being true to you. When your gut feeling tells you something, make sure to listen to it before it's too late.

The person tries too hard to make himself look better

If you feel that the person is always trying to make himself look better at the expense of the truth, then you definitely have a pathological liar in your hands. Pathological liars have that incessant need to come off better than other people and will lie about his or her credentials at every opportunity.

You find yourself sympathizing with the person's victimhood

A pathological liar likes it when other people sympathize in with him or her so if the person you're with stretches the truth to make it seem like he or she was the victim, it might be time to seek for professional help. Pathological liars will lie about both the good and the bad about their lives as long as it helps them achieve their motives.

The person has self esteem issues

Compulsive liars more often than not struggle with self-esteem issues and will exaggerate facts and details about themselves. While we all have the tendency to tell elaborate stories when we feel a bit unsure of ourselves, pathological liars will go to extremes to give themselves alternative lives or personas. This is the probably the reason why it seems like you don't completely know the person you're with most of the time.

You describe your life together as a roller coaster

This may sound a bit romantic, but if you're going to really think about it, would you really want to be in a relationship that can only be described as a roller coaster? All relationships will have their own highs and lows, but if you constantly feel like you're on the lows because of the lack or truth in your relationship, then it might be time quit the ride altogether.

If you notice any of these signs in the person you're with, you need to make a choice this early on. You can either remove yourself from the situation, or you can work on creating a new relationship dynamic. Either way, you need to remember that the choice is up to you. You have the power and control to turn your situation around. Don't allow yourself to get caught up in the other person's lies because it will only end in heartache.

Dealing with Emotional Manipulators and Pathological Liars

Dealing with emotional manipulators and pathological liars will require some painful changes, but you can always take the first step to ensure that you never have to settle for deception and emotional abuse again. Here are some tips to help you out.

Set healthy boundaries

You don't have to be available to everyone, especially if it's already interfering with your own life. Set healthy boundaries for yourself so you don't end up being a doormat to anyone. Once you set those boundaries, make sure to let the other person know about it.

Be your own defender

There are times when you'll feel like standing up for yourself isn't worth the trouble. This often happens when your thoughts are being dismissed or criticized. Always remember to stand up for yourself every chance you get. If you don't, no one else will.

Fill yourself up first

You simply can't give if you have nothing give. How can you give love if there's nothing left in you to give? This is why it's important that you learn to make yourself your top priority before you even think of getting into a relationship. When you make yourself your top priority, you're not just taking care of yourself, but you're also showing others your true value.

Take responsibility over your own actions

Quit playing the blame game and start taking more responsibility over your own actions and reactions. When you put the blame on others for how you feel, you're in effect giving them the power over your actions and reactions. Break free from this vicious cycle and remember that you're the only one who has control over your own life.

Express yourself

Don't let pent up emotions get the best out of you, especially if you're the emotional type. If you have any concerns, make it a point to voice it out. Talk it out with the person, or if you're more comfortable writing it down, express it in a letter. Keeping your emotions trapped within will only result in pent up negativity.

Revive and renew your spirit

All the dysfunction you've been dealing with has probably left you with an empty spirit. The only way that you'll be able to recover fully is by taking time and space for yourself. Don't feel guilty about taking a vacation for yourself if you think it's going to help you get your sense of self back again. if you can't revive and renew your spirit on your own, no one else can.

Your greatest weapon against manipulation is awareness. If you don't know how to recognize the signs, then how can you tell if you're already being taken advantage of? There's the tendency that you may become overcritical of yourself during this phase so don't beat yourself up for the mistakes you've made. Instead, use what you have learned to free yourself from the mess and work on starting over again. Promise yourself that you'll never play the role of the victim ever again.

Conclusion

Thank you again for reading this book!

I hope this book was able to help you to understand what manipulative relationships are and how you can take that next step to saving yourself from the heartache.

If there was one lesson that you should remember from this book it's that, while you can't be directly responsible for changing people, you however have the power to change yourself. Instead of directing your focus on how you would like to change that manipulative person in your life, it might be time to look to yourself to see what areas you still need to improve on

It might be hard to accept right now, but that person who keeps on lying to you and hurting you is never going to change. You don't have the power to change the manipulative person in your life because eventually, the choice is up to them. The best you can do now is change what you can about yourself and wait for a better path to reveal itself. You deserve to be in a healthy relationship – don't ever forget that.

The next step is to finally get out there and put into practice what you have learned. Now is the perfect time to take that step towards freedom.

Finally, if you enjoyed this book, then I'd like to ask you for a favor, would you be kind enough to leave a review for this book on Amazon? It'd be greatly appreciated!

Thank you and good luck!

Keep Reading For A Free Preview Of:

'Sociopath Exposed: Your Ultimate Survival Guide To Dealing With Sociopaths At Work, In Relationships, And In Life'

Chapter 2 - How to Do Business with a Sociopath

Perhaps the most ideal answer for this would be not to do business with them at all. If only life were that simple. The fact is that meeting a sociopath in the business world and in the workplace is very common. The most challenging thing perhaps is that unless the sociopath actually does something that can be considered as unethical, you cannot really file a complaint against them. There are two ways to deal with them: either you work around them or you find another job. The key is not to let their behavioral disorder affect your source of livelihood.

Signs that You are Working with a Sociopath

- ➤ The person provides you with superficial compliments and then criticizes you heavily.

- ➤ The person talks and acts in a condescending manner and exhibits a sense of superiority.

- ➤ He seems to exist in a fictional universe where his intentions and actions have no connection to reality.

- ➤ He switches topics randomly.

- ➤ The person shows micro-focus on things that interest him but have no connection whatsoever to existing organizational issues.

- ➤ He continuously weakens work progress by creating disorder, distraction, and destruction in the organization.

- ➤ He constantly blames other people for his negative behavior.

- ➤ The person displays contradictory speech and behavior.

- ➤ He spreads gossips and lies with or without apparent benefit to him.

> The person may display interest towards you at one time and then completely ignores you the next.

Dealing with the Corporate Sociopath

> It may sound funny but the fact is in order to deal with a sociopath, you must first learn to think like one. The first thing that you should do is to find out what the individual's underlying motivation is. Doing so will enable you to anticipate his moves. Just remember that sociopaths, unlike normal people, are not driven by the thought of "What is right." If you notice them doing something nice, keep your eyes open for an ulterior motive.

> You may engage yourself in one-on-one talk with the person to be able to understand him better. However, this should be limited to harmless small talk and must not include decision-making conversations. For meetings which involve a decision, ensure that there are other people around to act as witnesses or to direct important decisions.

> Sociopaths like to control the conversation. So be sure to speak up and maintain a neutral discussion.

> When speaking with the corporate sociopath, listen to him but always take his words with a grain of salt. Never believe in anything that you cannot personally verify. Working with a person with ASPD means you'll have to be aware of what's going on around you and continuously assess the current situation.

> Practice your flexibility. Sociopath colleagues will inevitably do something to mess up your efforts while you are making progress. Train yourself to adapt and develop your strategic thinking skills. Plainly put, make sure that you're always one step ahead of him.

> Make clever trade-offs. It is necessary for you to be able to determine the difference between what's important to the organization and what's important to the corporate sociopath. If you're in a position to do it, steer

the sociopath away from important projects and keep him occupied with other issues that will only create a minor impact on the company. Make sure to assign someone that you trust to support the person with ASPD with his tasks.

To check out the rest of "Sociopath Exposed", head over to the closest computer and visit the following link: **http://www.books4everyone.com/sociopath**

www.ingramcontent.com/pod-product-compliance
Lightning Source LLC
Chambersburg PA
CBHW060352290526
45791CB00004B/1645